Healing in a Word

George E. Samuels

iUniverse, Inc.
New York   Bloomington

Healing in a Word

iUniverse books may be ordered through booksellers or by contacting:

iUniverse
1663 Liberty Drive
Bloomington, IN 47403
www.iuniverse.com
1-800-Authors (1-800-288-4677)

Because of the dynamic nature of the Internet, any Web addresses or links contained in this book may have changed since publication and may no longer be valid.

ISBN: 978-1-4502-3531-0 (sc)
ISBN: 978-1-4502-3536-5 (dj)
ISBN: 978-1-4502-3533-4 (ebk)

Printed in the United States of America

iUniverse rev. date: 6/23/2010

Contents

Dedication

To a Mothers' love that is Healing
Thanks Ma!

Introduction

In the beginning there was the Word
Let there be Light
And the darkness disappeared
And there was only light.

A word can heal or harm. Best we use the healing words to heal ourselves and others by thinking positive thoughts and saying positive words.
It is our choice!

George E.

POETRY FROM THE HEART

Hearts linked to all reveal the state of health and wealth
Hearts heal when love reveals
Who you really are
Inside out
Hearts heal
And bodies reveal
What is on the inside
In daylight we see
Night we heal
Sleep and know you are well
The souls reveal
What is needed to be healed!

Hello

Hi
Called you
Hear me
Inside
Healing you
All the way
I am the healer
Not them
I know you
Do you recognize me?
I am the true doctor
Hear me now
All the time you think it is them
And it is me you doubt
Not knowing the truth
You lie to yourself
And they lie to you
Can they heal
Of course not
The cold
Flu
Cancer
Anything
No
I can predict
Can they?
No just guess
I am the one you should be seeing
Listening to
Hear me or feel my pain
Your body is mine
Not theirs
I cry you feel
I can make you cry if you don't listen
And make you smile if you do

I am the greatest Healer
See my light
My energy
Oh you doubt
Then we will see tonight
Gas out
Breathe in
Exhale
You can't do it
We are the one
Got it
Or you then d….(didn't)
Ok just kidding
Relax
Exercise
Eat right
But also remember I
I am the Real Healer!!

Heart Sounds

Ringing in the ear so loud that I can't avoid
Wonder why we shout
So quiet the ear
I wonder why I hear it in my heart
How is the noise from the crowd?
That makes a noise so loud
So quiet
I am listening with all my might
Only to hear what is light
I am listening
Can you hear?
Or have you shut the door
So no noise can be heard
Or what your heart have said
To you
To all
So speak or listen
But open the door so you can hear
Yourself
Out loud
I can hear you
I am listening
Loud I am
Quiet are you
Do speak up
Out loud
I am listening
Are you?
Wonder why you cry
Smile
Hearts speak out loud
Just open your ears and listen
You too will know what I am saying
To you
To all

Who will listen?
To my heart as it speaks
To you
Quiet, shhh
Listen
It is singing
You hear
If not you need to talk from the heart
And then you will hear
Yourself
Listen carefully
So you can hear you
And your heart
Making sounds!

Love

Life turns
For the better
For the worse
Me and you
Love
For loves sake
Make a love note
Beat the bush
Beat the wall
Search the stream
See where the love beams
Shines and strikes you
Is it in the heart?
Is it in the mind?
Or is love everywhere
My love is big
My love is huge
My love encompasses you
Does your love grow?
Where does it go?
Looking for love
Is not the answer
It is in front of you
It is facing you
Who do you love?
Does love love you?
My heart is full
Of love
Love you too
Can you love me?
When
Where
Who
How
Big love

Small love
Incessantly flowing
Love all is so easy
Replace the fear
Replace the hate
Replace the mean
With the love stream
From me to you
Where is my love
Or is it for you
Who loves?
Who hates?
Who hates to love?
Me you
All
We love and happy you love
We love you too
Love all
So they can see love
Love!

Mind, Body and Soul

Young
Yet so old
Mind
I cry
And wonder if it helps
My mind body or soul
It is important
To control
The mind
I mind my body
See the soul
My mind is ready
To heal
If it can rest
And let the mind
Go to its home
And then I can rest
But mind thinks of the body and soul
So old
Yet young
Go and tell the body
That it is whole
And the mind will bring the Soul
To make the body one
Body, Mind and Soul
That is the goal
The mind is minding the store
And the body is looking for more
But the Soul
Is young and yet so old.

Make Time for You

See the flowers grow
See the light on the horizon
See the mind glow
Make time for you
Bless the trees
Bless the people who try to please
But fall short
But only receive retort
From those who don't realize they do it all
No time for themselves
No time in the winter summer or fall
I make time
But you have no time for me
The children grow on their own
Only to see their dreams
That goes unrequited
Because they need time
Time to grow
Time we have
No time for those that are grown
Time for what we own
Or owe to each other
Waste not your life
Consider the waste of strife
You put me through
I put you through
Love is hard
Life is soft
I am happy
That you want more
But do we have time
For us
Without all the fuss
Time to smell
The flowers

Time for those we trust
Who take the time to come and visit us?
When we are tired
Of seeing them
But they take the time to show us
Their hearts filled with love with fire
I take the time
To see you as you are
And wish you look beyond the mime
The one act plays of life
That we keep going
To endless days
Busy too busy
To see who I am
Who you are
To me
And wonder if it is time
Or too time consuming to see
Or to take the time to see me!

Bananas of life

Too long
Too short
Too fat
Last a short time
But is nutritious for you
And for your health
Is it wealth?
The banana
Or is your life worth
What life has dealt
I like bananas
But a thing too good
Is too much
So I eat my bananas
Slow
And I don't worry
Knowing it is healthy
So my life is wealthy
From all that I consume
For my mind, my body
My life is full
Of bananas
I offer you one
But you can get your own
Mine might be sweeter
Because I pick mine
When ripe
Juicy
And I give my banana
Protection
From the wind
The rain
Life twist and turn
But my bananas remain the same
Yellow

Sweet ripe
Right on time
To find that
Satisfaction
I conceive
The nutrition I receive to make
Me whole
Control your appetite
A thing too good you shouldn't abuse
But bananas by the bushel
Chiquita I see
On my banana and me
We see bananas all night
All day
And know fruit is good
Bananas is beautiful and Chiquita is dancing
Because she knows it too!

HEALING

Up here
There we go
Trying to create a plan
When you know you can
Handle the healing needed
Be you and be me
Is all you need
To be
Love is a healing
Letting go of fear
You hear
Life is a healing
Let go of deaths grip
Holding you from living your life
Life is healing you
Now and forever
I am the healer
Who has come
To heal some
Or all who believe
In me
The Divine
In you and we
I am here to see you whole
Not a part of the fold
But one with the All
That is the goal
Life is like cheese
Melting away
Some with holes
Others stink
But the sweet fragrance of Light
And love can heal the aroma
Changing the shape of all that is
And is to be

So that you can be
Who you are meant to be
And they can heal their
Hearts
And become a part
Of the healers light
And might
Given to those who come with light
That is the healers light
That flows through them to you
With all the Divine's might
In and out of sight
Just look at the bright shining light and tell me
Who is to fight
what is in sight
Of those who can see
And know what is right!
The Healer is right in front of your eye
In your heart!

What a Fuss

What a fuss
You make
About nothing
I see the problem
Eye to eye
Mind searching for answers
Look inside to see
What the eye can't see
Wash your mind
And know it is clean and clear
Bright is the light
Look see it shines
Why you afraid to see
Are you blind?
Or are you hiding from the way
To the Divine
To help you see past
the blind Spot
You look to others
When I am in front of you
How come you cannot see
For looking?
I see what the problem is
You think this is all there is
I assure you it is not
But you trust not
The one who is here
Not in the blind spot
But in the temple of your mind
Where you don't visit
Because you are too busy playing outside
Come in out of the dark
Be a part
Of what is
And stray not to what is not

Looking good you think....
I see that it is superficial
Not deep
But deep is how high
Can you go.....
Climb the proverbial mountain
I am happy you will try
So you can succeed
To do
To be
All you can and do
All you can to help you me we
Out of this crag mire
And into the design you envisioned when you sleep
Dream the dream
Of all that is to be
So fuss if you must
Make a big fuss
Because you can't go quietly
And expect them to listen
They are inundated with white noise
And can't hear the scream from the cry
But they can see you smile
And know it is not you smiling
But us who try to reach deep and make them
Free from the fuss
In their lives
To be in the tranquility of the moment and
No longer live in the past
Fussing about while the future awaits them
And they fuss their life to realize later
Nothing was gained but the fuss
No need no muss
What I am saying is to listen
You must
Because it is all that is required
To be at peace and quell the fire

Rushing about in the mire
Understand the mountain awaits
So if you must fuss
Be about the heights
That awaits your climb up the ladder
To a place where fuss doesn't matter!

Left Out

High on the list is all that seems to be with it
All is not as it seems
Left out you think you are forgotten
We love you and you are in the mix
Wait till you hear the sound of the horn
Signally a new day
A new way to get home
We are the one who has come
And all is waiting to hear the noise that will be made
To signal a new day
Life is above and below
But many don't see the above
Only the below
Life is lived
And life is given to all
Living is great
But life is divine
Not the decadence many think it is.
Control is what is expected
But many out of control
Not realizing
All is tested
All is watched
All is graded
All is not ready
Some are most not
Because they don't
Know or understand
Life or control
Heart in wrong places
Mind not used
Emotions blazing
Why do you think
The mess is not to be overgrown
Like weeds

One needs to see the wheat not the chaff
Be wheat
Don't get the shaft
Life is growing
Heart is pleased
Heart realize the needs
Relax, all is
As it is to be
Be ready to be
See the world at peace!

Wife Call

All is abundant with the wife
All is abundant with life
All is abundant with love in the heart
Love is abundant
Love is flowing
In and out
Wife is waiting
To see much
You rest worry not
Much is given
Much is enough
Bless the heart
Bless the wife
Bless the time
Life is offering
So you can see the.......
The life with the wife!

Outside Agitation

Outside agitation is
Banging in my mind
Life's noise screaming
The name of healing
When they are making you sick
Healing is there
But ignored
Pills have side effects
But healing is real
Herbs abound
Down is up
Up is all the way on high
Mind is thinking wrong
Modern is not always the same
As traditional
But people sell more
To make you sick
Not well
Got the side effect
Now...
What do we do?
Agitate the rest
Peace inside was gone
Balance is a concern
That these chemicals make way
To travel the course but are not recognized
And the body now making a fuss
Inside
Rest can help but the agitation
Makes waste
We need natural remedies
So that the balance can make us at peace
We want to heal
But pills and surgery is illusion made real
It will help if needed but

We need to be still and understand that tied, pulled
And stretched is not the best
And pills can't solve rest
Just stop the noise stop the stress
Best to lay down and forget the mess
That got us here
That's best
Or you can live with
The agitation
And hope that pills will bless
It is not what is needed
All that is needed is a world blessed
With peace and rest
Quiet is the night
Being quiet is taking a rest
And love is the best
Happy is the dream of no agitation
And peace is the conquest!

Inner Peace

I am happy
I am healing
I am at peace
What is needed
Besides rest
Love is abound
My blood pressure is down
Life is unfolding
And I am growing
Life is peaceful
But comes a time
When the noise appears
Outside
I look and see
The people making the noise
Why are they here
Wow the world is at war
Noise everywhere
All the things I hold dear
Are going away
Finances are astray
My mind is thinking it is only a delay
That this is not real
It is all an illusion
That this noise is interrupting
I soar when at peace
But now am grounded
The ebb and tide is pulling
Me away
From the center
Of the pendulum
I don't want to be on the scale
Weighing in the balance
My brothers are warring
And all is not right at its place

Where we can all enjoy the best appeal
Or yield
Of our efforts
We must retain
The right balance
How is that to happen?
Of all the things in the library
No peace to be found
They say just be quiet
How so
I am looking for peace
I turn to the church
They screaming
Must be a problem
So I go home and see a glimpse
Of myself in the mirror
I see what I was looking for
Inside there is a place
Here peace resides
Behind the locked door
On the sofa
No on the mantle
In the kitchen
Oh the food is great
But the peace of food is gone
Once I ate
But then I fell asleep
Belly full
Still seeking
And realized I went to a place
That where I can be at peace
Inside
Inner peace!!!

Hey

Hey
What is the healing about?
Love
Is all that it is about?
Healing you from the pain
Being insane
From the life
I love
Heal me
My heart is hurting
Heal me
Peace
Love
Is this all it is about?
What about your heart
Heal
Love
Hate is out
Money is not what it is about
Love
Throws all of this out
You love
I doubt
Because you need the healing
The body
The mind
The life your kind
Of living
Getting caught up
In the vine
Webs in the mind
Traps
You thought
Of what is real
Illusions surreal

Be real
Heal
Lover
All heal
The life for you is a huge deal
But you can do
The impossible
The real deal
Yes
you can love
And heal
Best test
Is this what is bothering you?
Release yourself
Break the bars of imprisonment
To heal
Let it go
You reap what you sow
If you don't
Love
Heal
Then be real!

Begin

Begin
To make
The step
Toward
Healing
The old
Fashioned
Way
Pray
Move
To a place
Where
You can
Do it
Without
Vacillating
And
Know
That
The mind
Can
Do
Wonders
For you
If
You believe
In healing!

Believe

I am
You are
Healing
Those
Who come
To see
You and
Don't know
That they
Are better off
If they believe
In you and me
Because
They are being healed
Even if they can't see me!

Breathe

Breathe
And relax
Heal
And relax
Be
And relax
Be you
And relax
Be ready
And relax
We are healing
So relax
The day
Relax
The night
Rest and relax
Worry
Not and relax
Stress
No more
Relax
Just relax
And breathe!!

Righteous Mind

Believe
Me
I believe you
Mind right
Or wrong
Think long
Think wrong
Get it right
Suffer the consequence
Of your thinking
Got it
Think about it
Who is wrong?
Not them
You
Think right
All night
Doesn't help
Listen to the sound
Of the mind
Follow the thoughts
See what is wrong
Or right
Get it together
Now
Don't procrastinate
I am waiting
Still thinking
Of what
Me
You
Them
They
Can't all be wrong
Or right

Tonight
Think correct
Or you will become a wreck
Now do it correctly
Mind right
Then act correctly
And know that
When the mind is thinking
It can be right
Or you thinking wrong
Correct the mind
And you will be right on time
You know I am right
I think
My mind
Is thinking I am correct
So I will mind what I say
And correct what I think
Become in sync this very day
So I may be right just as I say!

Mending Your Fence

Life is under attack
Fences keep people out
Life is undersold
Life is making those bold
Why look across the fence
People want you to be on the other side
I am not ready to move outside
What life brings all together
Except the fence is in the way
Fences stand still day after day
Life can change
Fences stay the same
Minds can change but fences
Keep you the same
Fences can separate
Those that should be together
Fences help segregate
But you think like the fence
Separate
I knock down those fences
Don't cry
Fences signify
Stay on your side
But fences
Can make those who want to be together
To stay on the outside
Breathe on the outside
Breathe on the inside
Remove the fence from the mind
Don't you think it is about time?
Or are you caught up in the mime
Acting like you want to be together
But putting up fences everywhere
Now and forever
Relax the requirement

And move the fence
Mending the fence
Is not the same as ripping it down
But maybe you need time to come around
Lessons mend the fence or tear it down
The fence is the mind you seek
To clear a way to the problem
I say forget the mend
Don't bend it around
Just tear it down!

Internal

Life is internal
Externally we experience life
Life is out
In
Out of your mind
Excellent
To be
Life is alive
About you
About me
Get some
Or none
Healing is life
Energy
And sick is an illusion
You breathe
In and out life
Internal
External
Exhale
The things used
Finished
In and out
Gone
Internally you breathe
And heal
Love
Is healing energy
And part of your life
Is feeling
Is it real
Can you see it
Touch it
No
Because it is internal

Realize
It is real
Or is it illusion
I am You are
Know this!!!!

Balance

Life is on a scale
Weigh in the balance
Do you see where you are?
I am glad to measure
All that is in my life
And realize I am
In balance
Or not
Guess you have to know
That when you are out
You have to get back in
Getting in
Is easy when you know how
To change
And live that way
Then all seems to fall in place
Otherwise
It doesn't
And you wish it would change
But the scales
Swing to and fro
To help you
But it is way out if you don't realize
And the shock is
When you are out of balance
I try to make sure it comes back in
Balance so that I can
Do and be correct
And work
Play
Enjoy
All in balance!!

Peas and Butter

Love inside
Hope inside
Love outside
Love you
Why not
Peas and butter
Makes a difference
Peas and butter
On my plate
But can't eat
Filled with love
And peas and butter
I am impressed
That you love
Peas and butter
What about love
Outside
And inside
Love yourself
And we can eat peas and butter together!

Goodness

Good thinking
Good beginnings
Good endings
Good day
In every way
Good to be me
Good to you
Good we are here today
Good they are gone tomorrow
Good I am
Good you are
Good it is the time
For me
Good I recognize you
Good you came
Good I enjoy
It all
Good it is around
To enjoy
Good thinking
Goodness gracious!

Grant

Grant me the ability to see
If you are there
And I know you are
And I am
There too
But you
Need to see
Me around
And not act
Like I am not there
And realize
I am that I am
And you are
You
The high place is near
You and I are there with you
So let me see you
Shine and be the star
Glow brightly
So all can know you are here
Seal the mind and realize the heart is full
Of love
And I am
You know I am
You can do all
That you need
And all that they need
So that
The next can happen
And the next will be
You will be you
And they will know that you are here
Coming and going
Home!

Be Aware

Be aware
Of your life
Of strife
Things you bring to the game
Know how to play
I am aware
Of you
Are you of me
Name
The game
I play
Can you?
Be aware
The game is won
I am winning
Are you?
I am who I am
Who are you?
Be who you are
And I will be who I am
Everyday
Every way
And you?
What is it you're doing?
Don't know
Find out Love
I am sure
You are aware
Of what
I don't know
I know
What you should be aware of
And I know
Do you?
Smart then wise up

And don't repeat
The same old story
New day, new way
Are you aware
Of that
Fat chance
We know
We are aware
Are you?

Gift

Gift of giving
Is what we need
To you
I see the gift
Giving it to you
And wishing it was mine
I share
All that I have and can give
To you
I and you are the gifts
Of spirit
And we give
All we can to you
Can you open to receive it?
That which is a gift
To be received
Unconditionally
With all
That you get from others
Can you know the difference
Of the gift I gave you
Given to me
To give to share
And I am happy
To share with all!

The Band aid

Band aid on the problem
Heals
Or not
How do I know?
Can't see for looking
I am surprised
If it is not
Too scared to remove prematurely
But worried and want to know
How it is healing
On the way
Today or tomorrow
Can I peek?
Scared to stop the healing
Temptation is eating
At me
But I want to see if I am doing the right thing
No leave it in the dark
Be careful when I wash
Not to disturb it
Or to cause it to stop the process
I am glad I covered it
Because
Then it can heal on its own
Away from the germ
And germicide
And people touching it
Infecting it
With their notions
Or questions
Or apologies
About what happened
How and why
I am safe
From the crowd

I am healing
Waiting
It is 6 months
Is it done yet
No I can't look
I will wait and see
I am scared
To look
See if it is ok
Please look for me
I am happy
You came
See but don't disturb
Wait until
I think it is time
Then come and see for me
I would remove the bandage but
You know the air
Is full
Of whatever
I want it to be
Safe, in the dark
Away, from those who would infect it
Wait it is itching
Scratch it
Please for me
I need help
I don't want your help
It will do it on its own
Stop, don't tell me it is healed
It is doing its thing slowly
2 years still it is not time
I will try to take a look
No don't pull off the band aid
It might get infected
Ohhh it hurts
But there seems to be no pain

Only a memory like yesterday
Love it
Take it away
Now please
I can't take it anymore
Leave the band aid alone
Noooooo
Ok
I understand you will return
When I think it is time
But you are wrong
It is not healed
That is why I left the band aid on
There will be a scar if you don't leave it alone
Then others will see it and I will be embarrassed
That I removed the band aid
And didn't leave it alone
Ok go ahead
See if my heart is healed!

Health in a Hat

Health in a hat
Not all black
Or white
Colors are good
For your health
Wealth is many colors
Inside
Out
In food
Without a doubt
Heal the heart
Color it green
Color your mouth
Don't pout
Blue is not the color of the sky
Only
We need to see white
And heal
Golden opportunities are there
All around you
Pink and send to others
Yellow
Will keep you alive
And mellow
Orange a day keeps you alive
And apples can make you survive
Clean the colon
And then they will be golden
So violet are your mind
And purple is not your eyes
But you can see it in the wine
Drink and be merry
Water doth a bath don't be weary
So rest and you will get up fine
In the morning!

Badge

Badge of all that is here
Gone is the marks we wear
Swear you care
And we will dare
To be with all you can compare
Life is success
Failure is not a thought
Or is death forethought
I am the light that beams
In your eyes
I am the husband that talks to the wives
About all they have experienced
And all they will experience
Because they share
All that they hold dear
Hearts soar
Even when they are bored
They lift up the children
And render
Them women and men
When they are old
Enough to see what is silver and what appears to be gold
They are the ones who walk
And talk the talk
Hoping they will be
Al they can do and be
And be and do
To me to you
And all they see
Meet, read
And the time to tear
The mind from the thought
Only to find out there is more
Is the being that you can see?
You and me

And know we are one
In the same
Game
We play
While others are part of another frame
Pictures are a thousand words
Then why we scramble our thoughts
Things are there
That we have met
And discarded
Like old cards
And so is the mate
Too weary for the date
And shows us the gate
And we cry
Don't know why
But it's do or die
Trying to please
You or is it me
I don't know can you see
Us, we, me
Crisis over, time to go
And we will be happy
We came
It's not the same
Without us!

Life Rounds

Life is around
New
And old
It is true
Life is
Around
You
Me
All
But life
Is lived
Not death
Life
Is yours
Given to you
For you to do
Life is around
And you should live it everyday
In every way
So you can be
And feel
Alive
Around
You and
Others
Who live
And do
You can feel alive
Not death
Live for the day
Live for the moment
In every way
Say and do
What you came here for you
To do

Destiny
Is in front
Past is already lived
Believe in the life you live
Now
Tomorrow
Presently
And then tomorrow
We can
And will
Be alive
Not just survive
But living our life!

Heart, Love or Not

Love or not
Tie the knot
But not with my heart
I say
You may
See me or not
That is why I am not
Seeing my heart
Love you
Love me
And see
If I care
Or dare
To love you back
I attack
Your sensibilities
I tie the heart
In a knot
And ask that you love me
Or not
But don't hide your heart
From me
Or you
I will love you too
If you trust that I am
And you
Are
Or not
Love is the heart
I open
You open or close
Or not
But you can love with your heart
Or not
Love

Me or
I will not
Love you
Too
With all my heart!

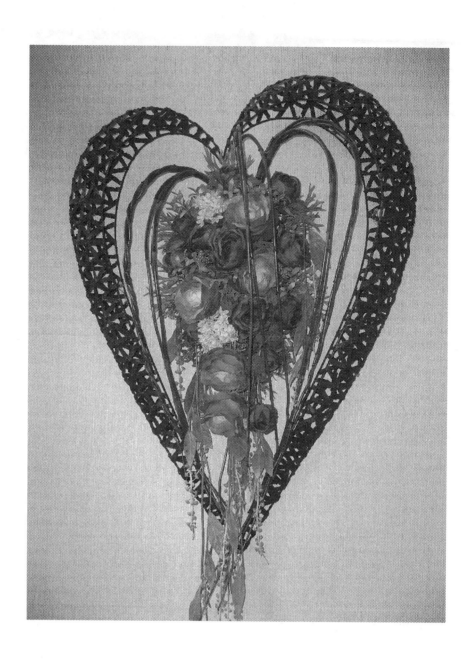

Lessons in health

Wonder where my health went
While I watched the TV
Was it there?
Where did it go while I was sleeping
Did it creep out?
I guess
Without a doubt
Life is a lesson
On health
What is the real wealth?
Money or health
I wonder
Who decided
On the former
On the latter
Only to be right
Or wrong
You can try with all your might
Can't get health
With your wealth
I treasure health
For it is without question
A major lesson
On what comes first
The egg
I wonder
Don't doubt the chicken
Had to be healthy
Not wealthy
To lay a egg
Without any money
I can keep my health
And keep my honey
Mind you health
Or health will be on your mind

When it is gone
And you will not be given it or reborn
So renew
Your effort
To maintain a method
To keep your health
And you will have learned a valuable lesson
On health!

Worry

For what
Do I worry?
I worry about you
You worry about me
Why don't we relax
Worry about
Nothing
That sounds right
I relax
And think of you
I wonder do you
Do the same
It is wise
To learn
How to do the same
I rest
Do you?
I wish you would not worry
About you
Let me worry
I know how to do
And then I can
Know you are ok
And then I can rest
And not worry
About
You too!

Realize He is Brave

Brave
Is the one who
is sick
Realizes
He can heal
Realizes
He needs to heal
Realizes
He is willing
And ready
And want
To heal
Realizes
That all it takes
Is mind
Realizes
The divine
Thought
That all is One
And healing
Is Divine
Brave is the one who accepts
The truth
And then realizes
He can change his life
Heal his life
Realizes
It's in his hand
To be
Or not
Then takes
Action
Realizing
The only
And begins

The journey
Brave and ready
To do battle
And win!

Be Able To Do Work

Being able to do work
Requires you to be strong
Not weak
Not sick
To be healthy
Remain strong
And know that
You can deal with all that is brought to you
And be able
To do what you need to
We be who we are
By the time
We realize that
Our health
Is the true bless
That we received
We can't complain
If we haven't taken care
Of our self
And then try to run
When walking is all we can do
And we are laid up in the hospital
For a rest
Life teaches us to be aware
That we need to remain strong
And to do work
But work can be accomplished
When we remain strong
And do what is required
Eat exercise and rest
Trouble will not come nigh your door
If you realize
You are the blessed
In disguise
To be able to do all you can do

And remain ready
To be and take care of you
Then all who rely on you
when you are ready and at your best
Be strong
And do what you need to do to accomplish your work
And do what you know is best
To remain strong
Go get the rest
Then do your work
Do your best!

Teach Them

Teach them
To rest
Best
For your health
Rest
Best
For the mind body soul
Toll
On mind
And body
Is much
Too stressed
Contest the attitude
To think
You don't need rest
I am whole
At best
When I eat right
Exercise and rest
Sleep
It pays dividends
At best
For your whole life
And when you
Are out
Strife is the lesson
Not to win
But will lose
If you don't learn to rest
Don't be a fool
Relax
It doesn't make you lax
It energizes
You to take on more
And less

And be able to run
With the rest
Who take heed
And relax and rest
Be aware
You need your rest!

Ready or Not

I am ready
Are you
Improve
Forgive
Leave
The nonsense
Go home
Behave
Realize
You
Are being
Tested
Ready or not
Go
Home
Stay
Do
Don't
What are you waiting for?
Me
I am waiting for you
Are you ready?
Smile
Hate
Love
Peace
War
Me and my heart
You and your heart
Hate
Or love
Make up your mind
Let it go
Worry
Stress

Anxiety
We love
You love?
Or hate?
Love
Ready or not
Be
Ready!

Box

Box
Inside
Outside
Who is in the box
Your mind
Your heart
Your body
Inside
Outside
Where are you
Don't you know,
Or care
You are in where?
The box
Out
Don't know
Ask
Inside
Out
Outside in
Box
No box
Sky
Limits
In the box
Outside
Limit is the sky
Why don't you know,
See
Ask
Or care
We know why
You should too!

Reasons They Want To Be Free

Health reasons
Love reasons
Hate reasons
Life reasons
Anger reasons
All reasons
For life
Living
Being
We live
To love
Not hate
To be in the life
Not dead
To the world
To the family
To the people around us
But they must live too
Life is the same for them
And they live for us and them
And all is the same
Just different
People
In different places
Loving
Living
And hoping that we let them live
And be
And love
Too
Not become property
And then we place ownership tags
On them
Their lives
Their hearts

And become the
Lord and master
Of they....
Who want to be free!

Breath

Breath
Of life
Breathe out all the strife
So we can sigh
And feel alive
Breath is the way
To live
Long
Short
Deep and wide
Do you breathe in the chest?
This is ok
But to breathe deep is best
And life will be strong
As it is to be
For you to live
From the air you breathe
And the life you conceive
When new life appears on this plane to breathe
Its first breath
Love and breath is connected
To the health
And death is connected to the lack of the breath
Young old breathe deep as you can
And life will course its way through the veins
So you can remain
Young and bright with life's flame!

Healing Hands

Healing hands
They touch
They are wide
Long tall
Short
Skinny
Fat
Nothing they lack
Healing hands
Darn aren't they for all
We heal
With our mind
Touch with our hands
Create with our bodies
Perfect unions and whole
Beings
That can see
Feel
Touch
Our hands
Hearts reach out
Hands are connected to our hearts
Without our hands
How do we touch their hearts
And feel
The pulsation of their thoughts
on their goals
Life is everywhere
Even in our hands
Healing energy flows from the heart
Through the fingers
Of the mind
We count five
The fingers give life
They take life out of mothers

To be revealed to the world
They love
And hit hard
To reach their point
To bring home the energy of love
that can only be touched by my hands
to your heart
Murmuring love
And forgiveness
If I squeeze too hard
Hands can control the destiny
And healing the future
And hold all that is dear
And let you know that the Divine does care!

Pills

Pills for what
Ill for what
Pills make you sick or well
Life we dwell
Or to make us whole
Physical beings need to heal
Pills may help but the side effect
Can make you ill as well
Who needs secondary problems?
When they take pills that are supposed to cure but instead add to
Your problems as well
Natural healing is a herbs job
Pills is not natural but chemical
So it is important for you to know this as well
Pill spelt p-ill is a lesson we must take as we-ll
So try herbs because they will make you feel swell
Life is natural and chemicals are not
So do not take unless you understand all the side effects
And know what is and what is not
That makes you whole and well!

Mind

Mind needs work
We think we know
But don't
Mind needs work
Body gets it all
Mind just is there hiding
Standing tall
We think we know
It all
Mind needs work
Especially if you want to heal all
And including your self
You need to learn how to delve
Into the mind
To do
Mind needs work
For you
To be you too
I know the body needs to heal
The mind needs to yield too
Depending on what you are wanting
From the body
If it doesn't it will take it
From the mind
Go and come
Begin
And begin again
Because it starts in the mind
Before you see it in the body
Then it appears
And disappears
When you think it is all done
Only to return where it begun
Again and again
Can't get rid of it

Because the mind needs work
Starting in the mind
Going to the body
Then the mind will help
It not to return to the body again
Heal the mind
Heal the body
Then the mind will work
And you won't need to work on it again!

Healing life

Love
Heals
Life
Strife
Being
Love
Heals
Heart
Right
Wrong
Top
To bottom
Life is
Healing
After
You realize
Love
Heals life!

Be Love to Heal Love

Love you
Hate you
So what
I don't feel good
I love me
Hate you
Feel bad
Why I am sick
To be or not to be
Love
Hate
In the same place
I want love
You want hate
We can't be together
You hate
In the past
You hate the last
I love
I love that's my task
Completed
And in love
My love is strong
Your hate is strong
Why love to do hate
When you can love
I am well
You sick
I love my health
I love
You can too
Be love
Release hate
And love wins
Health is better

Heart has changed
Why?
I love you
You love now, things can improve
You can be you
I can be me
We love
Heal us
Heal our relationship
All is well!!

Innocent

I am innocent
How come it is a sin?
Body knows full well
I didn't do anything
Why harm me
When I did nothing
I am innocent
Betray me
Then stay away
For it is not the way
For you to behave
Trust the spirit
And know that you have spirit
You know you innocent
So why admit to wrong
You learn and know you are not forgone
You need to forgive
And chose to live
Innocent
That is if you know you are a deficient
Of the truth
The truth is
Not a lie
Beside
You know you are divine
Look within
See who is at fault
And don't be distraught
When you find out
You are innocent
And what is wrong is your thinking
And when you learn do the right thing
And be forgiven
And forgive those who are not innocent!

Elemental

Elements
Five or six
Seven
We are all of them
Natural order
We spend our lives
Being
The elements of order
All is in order
Balancing the universe
Of natural order
It seems that we
Don't realize we are made up of
All the elements
In Nature
And we represent a balance
Of those things
That brings good health
Wealth to well being
And all is in natural order
Of things being
In and out of disorder
And we keep to this
To resolve and re-order
Needing balance
And we move to make sure the scale is balanced
And wellness appears
As a part of the elemental order!

Washing

Washing the world
Won't make it go
Bathing the body
Won't make it whole
You can lie and steal
But it won't affect your soul
If you think
You can go to the church
And say 10 Hail Mary's so
Washing is cleanliness
Telling the truth
Is next to holiness
But a clean body won't make you a holy soul
Wash away the sins
And don't commit to more
Is what you are trying for
So wash and know when clean
It can be seen
By those who have washed their sins
And now are on the path
that will help them sow as they reap
Deep is the wash
Sow is the place
Win is the way to
Walk the path
Where there is no water
Wine doesn't go to waste and people dress
To impress not their friends but themselves
Life is in constant wash
And know that you are clean
On the outside or in
In between
Is not the place to be
Clean in and out don't matter
Clean out and in may be in the mire

We need to clean and wash
Our thoughts
Our mouths
And bodies
So our spirit can shine brightly
As a car on a Sunday
On our way to church
To be with those we appreciate
Or choose to deceive
That we are clean to the bone
Body spirit and soul
Wash you your mind
Wash your heart
And all in between
So from looking it can be seen
That you sparkle inside
Better than a car cleaned and sheened.

Global is the Warming

Global is the warming
Heart is aligned
With all that is
Healing those that are cold
Inside, outside
and in their soul
We blame the boy and the girl
but adults caused this problem
Global is the warming
Melting ice and cold
Snow is going and water is warming triple fold
It is time to see what the problem is
And not lay blame
Using the same old excuses
To insure monetary gain
Healing the planet will take all
Not only the ones who created this
But those who are seriously committed to success
Global warming is not the problem
But bad men polluting
And blaming it on everything but their misbehavior
Doing certain folks favors
How much more the looting
Before we see global warming
Is the only way to correct what they are doing
Healing the problem
Can only happen when you know the cause
And willing to heal this without
Counting the losses
Of what you are producing for the bosses
Global warming is healing
Correcting the problem that is revealing
Mistakes made without thinking
The consequences of actions
That is making this reaction

It is time to see what can be done
But blame isn't the name of the game
But solid action
That will help us all
Not more talk and more prizes
For those who really don't care what happens
Life is going on
Global warming is continuing
And more rhetoric is forming
But the pollution keeps growing
So stop talking
And heal global warming
By actually doing
If you can come out of the cold
To see what is going on!

Rest

Rest
Best
Doing less
Can help
You rest
Mind active
Blood boil
Burning the midnight oil
Less
Is best
Rest crucial
Not to be taken superficial
Life is on
Death is off
The table
Rest so you can be able
To do
Move
Live
Be at your best
Adequate must rest
Life money
Is work
For all
Trying to be the best
Get all they can
If allowed
They would never rest
Be aware
I am resting
So I can do all I can
Then I will be strong
Tall
And ready to do all
That is required for me to stay out of the mire

Because I am so tired
Be aware
Life is full of rare
Opportunity
To do if I am not tired
But care to get my rest
And then can handle all life's test!

Waking Up

Waking up
Asleep
We see
Not what is required
What we are supposed to see
We think it will go away
But it won't
It is
It don't
Go away
Why we say
It hides
And appears another day
I am sick
I am well
I know this
From what I can tell
Look
Be awake
See what it is we are supposed to
We need to look
Notice
What is on the surface
Lying deep
So hidden
It can't speak
But when it does
It screams
You didn't
Listen to me
Now you must
Need to pay attention
That was the intention
Do I have your attention
No then I will when you are in the hospital

Awake
Sleep
You will know
Or sow the reap
Be aware
I am where your secrets keep
You awake
When you are supposed to be sleep
Awake and know we need to acknowledge me!

Become

Become new
Old
Young
Old
Sold
On ideas
Of youth
Young
Bold
Sold
On ideas of old
Young
Being bold
Old feeling young
How are you
Being undone
Which age is it
I know
The old grow
The young get old
Sold
On vitamins
Herbs heal
Vitamins cost a great deal
Cheaper than medicine
But who wins
The undertaker
Deduct the cost
Of a funeral
And don't smoke
Heal
The mind
And the body will be set free
Your ass will follow
Grow

Young
Not bacteria
Or diarrhea
Pay for the organic
Poison is in the land and trees
Go green
Get lean
Fat ass can't fit
But you can get fit
Don't have a fit
Kiss
Love
Hate is not the order of the day
Peace
Heals
War steals
The young
And the old
From your family
And all those
Who don't know
Any better
Realize you are health
And wealth
If you take care
And become aware!

Color Me

Color me with your light
Color me from head to toe
I am a color
You are colors
Health is a color
Colors reveal health
Wealth
Sickness
We are the color
Of vitality
Love
Hearts
Wrapped
Totally with Spirit
Intelligent
Soulful
Strong
Light
We are the color
Of light
Prisms bend
Light infractions
Showing many colors
Of whom we are
Can be
Are not to be
Light shine
Darkness cannot comprehend
The light
The color
Our might
Choose who you are
The color
And the type
You want others to see

Believe and know
You are to receive
Light and color!

Envelope Please

Greatest symptom
Greatest cure
Greatest medicine
Greatest side effect
And perhaps greatest relapse
Greatest machine
Lean and mean
Greatest doctor
Of them all
Greatest plastic surgeon
Taking a fall
Plastic time
Bomb and all
More here today
Gone tomorrow
So is my color
Greatest tits, ass
To boot
Greatest cast
War chest full of loot
Ask Michael
150,000 per month
You're dead because
He is on a phone call
Greatest pain of them all
After you have taken a fall
On the stairs, bathroom
We assume lost footing, grip
After a sip
And a lot of lip
Greatest pain killer
Killed
Another prescription filled
Greatest poem ever written
Healed the sick

Good riddance
Greatest rip of them all
Called health care
Who they care for
Pharmaceuticals and bankers
That's all
Greatest medicine abuse
That's all and more
Biggest mistake and foul up
But don't want to pay malpractice
And you took the wrong leg
And called it practice
Ruin the tits
And call it the greatest fruits evermore
Cost some tits, ass and
Their life is no more
Lick your life away
So you can say
You have the greatest waist
Today
Greatest trick
Using old people and the sick
To make fortunes so slick
Is all a joust
Or is it HMO's
The greatest savior
Since slice cheese
Please don't make me sneeze
Just pass me the bills—
Oh the envelope please!

Health Wise

I am health wise
Are you
Love is
Health wise
Hate is not
Peace is health wise
War is not
Fighting doesn't improve the health
Money helps
But it can buy things
Not health
Otherwise
The rich would be healthy
And not die
Money is the way to pay
When you sick and go to the doctor
But that is not health wise
Health wise is preventive
Eating
Sleeping
Exercising
Relaxing
Being
Seeing
You are healthy
And knowing
To not do
What makes you sick
See in your life what you do
Is it health wise?
Be health wise
Or wise up!

Love's Healing Power

Love's healing power
Flows like water
Healing
Seeking
And filling all the holes
That is needed
To be filled
To be healed
To be corrected
Changed
To show love's healing power
Inside
Outside
And it knows no color
No one can stop it for long
For its power
Is stronger that the mighty river
Longer than the deep sea
Mightier than the warriors sword
Swifter than the bird in flight
And sharper than the point on the principals pen
Now and then
And it gives
Without asking
Who loses who wins
It is strong
And it is for the weak
And will conquer the war
Hero and more
For it is tall and wide and equal on both sides
Of the world
And whispers to us all
To partake and fill
Our hearts
As hearts will

And share what we can't spend
Now or then
With those who cannot extend their hearts
and see that we all are a part
And can heal
Those in need
Of love
And to plant a seed
That can burst into a flower
And grow into
Life's healing elixir
Love is life's healing power!

Healing In a Word

Love
Light
Bright
Be you
Love you
Love all
Life
Heal
Relax
Positive
Free
Mind clear
Love you dear
I am aware
Rest
Peace
Release
Let go
Get home
Don't worry
Laughing
Be happy
Divine
Hearts say love
From you to me
Words do heal
Speak your healing words!